Bridge to

MW00478781

Published in the United States of America

Written by Sandra L. Gibb, 2022-

Bridge to Awareness/ Awakened Insight for Child and Adult/ words by Sandra L. Gibb/ Illustrated by Sandra L. Gibb and Harrison Bell

ISBN 978-0-578-39920-1

ISBN 978-0-578-39920-1

90000>

9 780578 399201

Sandra L Gibb

Enjoys being of support in bringing awareness to child and adult. She mastered considerable expertise in her Spiritual gifts along with intuitive massage, healing gift of Reiki, spiritual and life coaching and Hypnotherapy.

Sandra has always been a people-oriented person and her focus on the East/West fusion of health services has included stints in the education arena with schools, coaching sports, a past business owner of travel and a graphic illustration company called, "Window Designs."

She enjoys Arts, outdoors, hiking travel, singing, dancing and the pursuit of new opportunities that align with Sandra's aims of regenerating body, mind, and Spirit.

Harrison Bell

Intuitive caring with deep insight, now in his teens. He enjoys art, symphony, outdoors, water activities, technology, also with interests in his studies, friends, and family.

Harrison's drawings have been Divinely guided for this book. The drawings evoke a person to look within the world we create. The cover of the book is Harrison's creation of "Holding the Universe and Time in Hand."

"Awareness in Balance"
"Living one's full potential to a higher understanding of truth and love."

This book is dedicated to life's expansion in all.

Awakening into Higher Consciousness

1

Awakened

The summer day was sunny and warm with a slight breeze in Ensenada, Baja California. My family, aunt, uncle, and cousins enjoyed time camping on the upper sandy area to the beach. I remember back so clearly to that camping trip. I had seen a dead fish on the shore, not too big for me to pick up and carry. My older sister and younger cousin were with me, enjoying the soft, smooth waves, lapping up onto the beach. I recall saying to my sister, "let's chase daddy with the fish." Her answer was "NO!" Thinking to myself, that was an odd response to hear. I picked up the dead fish anyway and had my cousin, who had just turned three, and I, a month shy of 4 years old, followed me as I started to run around my dad with the dead fish. At that moment is when my spiritual awakening started. Life outside of me seemed to stop for a few moments as I experienced this awakening within. I could see, feel, hear, taste, inner knowing, energy sight, and all the clairvoyances.

My dad's energy and thoughts were dangerous to my cousin and I for our well-being and safety. From that day forward, I always put up protection around me. How did I know to protect myself? I could feel instinctively with inner knowing and trust.

As we were running around my dad, the message I heard so clearly was to get out, to run up the sandy embankment.

Telepathically answering back to the knowing within, I said, "my legs are too short to run up the sandy embankment and that he would, for sure, be able to prevent our escape." So, I gave trust and faith we would be protected.

We finished running around my dad, which at that moment, I dropped the dead fish and grabbed my cousin's hand. We ran away from the sandy barrier and up to the campsite. At that point, I always kept my guard up whenever my dad was around.

Interestingly, I don't recall ever talking about that day or any other event of energies or voices to my mom or anyone else as a child. I trusted in the power and spiritual counseling that surrounded me. Whenever an energetic urgency came into play, I would feel this presence, which would help me be in the moment, give it up, and received by words or energetically knowing what to do.

2

Fear

How many times has your child voiced a fear, a knowing, and you blew it off? Or they had invisible friends, past life experiences, for example, saying, "Mommy, I knew you before." How about not yet meeting a cousin until they see a picture and your child gets so excited and says, "that's my buddy"! Or picking up a rose quartz stone, looks at it, puts it to his heart, and then puts the crystal down all at the age of 18 mo.? Ever wonder if your child can read your mind? Do you ever think something is very wrong with your child!!! Really? Have you forgotten about your Spirit? We are Spirit experiencing through a body.

Now is a time in all lives for truth and remembering.

Is fear blocking your receptiveness of higher awareness? You may call these children overly sensitive, introverts, off-the-wall active, uncontrollable; the list can go on if you live in fear.

Fear of forgetfulness, fear of media, fear of your reactions, fear of what family, friends, or people might say.

No better time than now to start communicating and talking with your child. Talking without belittling, be nonjudgmental, release your fear, and be without punishment. Your child is more connected to the Spirit world of Truth and Love, yet how many times do we squash their creativity just by not learning from them?

If we allow children through their beautiful raw innocence and connectivity to remind us of our inner child, how creative and loving we can once again see ourselves as the I am.

Peace

"Open your heart.

Shine Divine Love.

Embrace the experience.

See with amazement,

The world within."

Peace

&

Love

3

Experienced

A funny situation happened to me in third grade at lunch recess, baseball time! One of the boys from my class who liked me was also playing baseball. One of my girlfriends told me he was going to kiss me (my intuition told me that was true). When my turn to bat had approached, this young boy came up to me and kissed my cheek. What did I do? I went and told my teacher. With a smile on her face, she said she would talk to him. Reflecting on that time, what I wanted and needed was to be asked how I felt that incident affected or bothered me.

Also, what I thought would be the best resolution to kindly set boundaries, not to let others take advantage of a situation. She was a great teacher, yet, I needed that guidance.

Adults bring value to your child's abilities. Do you treat a child or person as not knowing, trusting, or giving them the tools to think and feel (which inspires creativity), mainly because you think you can do it faster, better, without a mess and stress.

Then think, my friend, how much you lose in regaining your connection to Spirit.

Release your tension, increase laughter, joy, give and receive hugs, be filled with inner peace, higher healthy boundaries, and enjoy your creative productivity, knowing how to paint your canvas in this experience of life.

"To gain the freedom is to relinquish the ego" You might be saying, "Whoa, too heavy!!!"

No problem. You can use this easy tool every time you start to dim your Divine Light by uncreative thoughts and actions, you know, like fear.

"I desire and command memory to keep my heart space expanded throughout all creation with healthy loving boundaries, for my higher good. Thank you."

If saying those words feel right, use them. Otherwise, search your Divine soul for what feels best for your highest good.

Attune

All Matter is Energy

A time of deeper connection is happening within and through you.
You are a spiritual being having a human experience.
Attune your vibration with your higher consciousness, healing is
found within you.

4

Connection

Childhood was interesting, as I observed with an awareness. I came from a family of 9, two adults, seven children. My mom would teach us to see shapes in the clouds and appreciate the vast beauty in the world. Like many families, we had our ups and downs. Yes, I could sense discord in individual persons, places, and things, yet I did not understand my abilities and gifts as I do now. When I am not in the presence of just being, that is when my connection is low. That is when I let fear and worry, which comes in many forms, control my life, I feel lonely. Why is this? It would be I have cut my Light of Connection with Creation. I have put up a veil, forgetting the Universe has my back. I allowed the ego to think it was the only thing that could help. When ego comes in, it is a time of awareness. Now let go and trust in the Divine Intelligence that always has our back and wants the best for us. Divine Light is our guide.

I ask all to allow children to ask questions without fear. Teaching them we are all unique. All have a purpose, and only they know what that purpose is by staying connected to Spirit, in trust, faith, Love, and non-judgement of self or others.

Just think of your families (also friends like your family), all those unique and indifferent personalities under the same roof! Different opinions, desires, hopes, fears, the list can go on, but each one has its purpose. My mom would say you can be whatever you desire. That is good. The other key here is example and support. Support is by teaching how one can learn and gather the tools to make healthy choices that will propel one to and through their growth of purpose.

How do we get there? Fear not to embrace the events of failure, for they are also your successes. We learn by trial and error, yet we need to embrace the possibilities, see the facts, let go of emotional drama to know which direction in life we are following. Become aware of what feels suitable and sound from the heart. This way, we can choose if it is for our higher good at that present moment. We can only live in the present. At that moment, we can heal the past, change the future, find peace in the now for the highest good for ourselves, and create in itself.

Feel

"Sense the energy of Earth.
Her love, life and beauty always supporting, always listening and
teaching. She never judges but always works at balancing the living
atmosphere for life.
How is the balance in yourself? Can you still see beauty and goodness among chaos? Does judgement block your
perception of truth?
Step away into nature. Feel the love that is showered upon all life.
You are Beauty, Spirit, and Love.

5

Feelings

What causes self-doubt? I turned five when I found out my cousin, who had just turned four, got $5 for her birthday. I asked my mom, "could I have $5 for my birthday?" She said, "ask your dad." At that moment, I felt doubtful, yet, I wanted $5 for my birthday; after all, I was older by one year. So, I went to my dad and asked, "Can I have $5 for my birthday?". "Oh yes," he asked that doubtful question (at least in my mind!) "Why do you think you should get $5 for your birthday?" I said, "It is my birthday, and my cousin got $5, and she is younger." His answer was, "I don't know." I let it go, at least I asked. My birthday came and yahoo!! I got $5. Was that my choice because I wanted $5 for my birthday or because my cousin got $5 for her birthday? Yes, it was because my cousin got $5! I had let my ego control my emotions. Better to gain awareness than never knowing.

"Ask, and you shall receive."

You will always get an answer that is best for you at that time. Stay in a higher vibration of Love and Worthiness. The key is to let go, have faith, trust, Love, and know the need in your life will be yours for the highest good and at the right timing.

Becoming into awareness is energy; it is growth; it is higher intuitiveness toward your purpose.

There are many things in my childhood I am unable to recall or choose to identify. It is part of being aware and living with my family life's ups and downs. As a child, I remember praying for my sibling's souls. Why? I was not receiving the information to know why for I was not aware I could ask. I learned to trust using prayer and an open heart to guide my feelings.

I mention being in awareness. Let me explain my outlook. At times I would be quiet in the sensing energy and connected with Spirit. To some it might seem as being zoned out, a know it all, too young to know, or overly sensitive.

My outlook had an intense caring with a divine feeling of Love in my heart. So, when a child's feelings get hurt, it is accurate. Do your inner child's feelings get hurt when you forget to nurture yourself with Love, forgiveness, compassion, and thankfulness?

We are Love itself, manifesting to and for the higher good. We are a canvas of events, color (Light and dark), choices, lines, curves, shapes, textures, energies, vibrations, seen and unseen, the creation within the creation, and the coming into awareness. Life's ups and downs teach us to remember where and who we are, always in the embrace of Divine Love and Guidance.

6

Questions

Oh my, ups and downs? My learning experiences by some could seem scary. Unless you are experiencing the phenomenon, it is hard to know how one would take empathic understanding. Remember the Ouija board? That was very frightful to me. I was in grade school when my older sister and I asked the Ouija board questions.

My question was, "Who was I going to marry?" A likely question for a young girl, right? Well! The first name was the same as a neighbor across the street, no way!!!! We asked some other questions, and then I said it was stupid. It came back saying some words that shocked both my sister and me. We didn't know how to spell those words, but we knew once written …hmm, let's say we realized we allowed a bad spirit to come through. At that moment, I threw the board away and told my mom. She had no problem with me getting rid of it, which surprised me. Note: At this age, I had no idea my mom was also intuitive and psychic. She was silent about acknowledging that information to me until I got older.

My life started in the 50s, not knowing about spirituality as ESP. Being taught in religion in that decade, you had to abide by many unnecessary rules, which I questioned even at a young age. Only helping you see that not listening to your heart, your inner Light can get blocked.

My mom was invited to a friend's wedding and could not go because she was not of the same religion. I had asked my mom why? She said the Church forbids going to a wedding outside the faith. I remember stopping a moment and checking within my Spirit and responding to my mom, "Did not God make us all?" She said, "well, yes." Without a moment lost, I replied, "well, if ever I get asked to go to anyone's wedding, even if they are not of the same Faith, I'm going to go!" Yes, parents, listen to your children and hear what they say. Their answer to a searching knowing may be in what comes out of their young mouths.

Hmmm...... a thought. When did you start killing your Spirit? We judge too quickly without hearing the lesson. How did you feel when I asked this question? What kind of book is this? Ready to throw it down? Fearful to what you might hear, learn or feel threatened by; it might change your so secure bolted thought and belief?

Oh, I know I have been there. It's all fear-based.
No one can force your opinion to change unless you allow the change. So, in teaching your child, do you kill their Spirit? Wow!!! What the heck are you saying?

Think for one moment in your childhood that you had a thought or feeling, and you voiced it only to be told, don't think that way! Maybe said that's crazy talk, and don't let others hear that or takes you to some form of doctor and treated like you were out of the norm. Maybe felt at that moment all life pulled out of you and that something is wrong? Why?

Because of the inflected thought from another, especially someone who is supposed to be supportive, loving, and non-judgmental?

Stillness

"Still but thy mind
allow my sense of awareness betroth to my
purpose and bring to me an
open heart from the sea of Love"

7

Gathering

To all sensitive children, be not afraid. Instead, ask questions. Truly listen, and support in Love and non-judgement. Find the information needed to become informed and gain more wisdom.

Do you know what is an Empath?

Spiritualist? Medium? Astrologer? Crystal or Indigo child? Psychic? Mystic? Oracle/Tarot card reader? One who Channels? Clairvoyance? Intuitive? Telepath? Body Code/Emotional Code Release therapist? One who sees and speaks to spirits? The lack of knowledge and understanding sets the wheels into fear. We All have the ability to these gifts eventually, yet our life here on Earth was for learning, helping, giving, receiving, forgiving, gratefulness, and being in oneness, Love eternal.

You are no better or lessor in the Creator's design. Overcome self-judgment, and release the inner fear. Become aware and allow your child to express, so we have the seeds of

Love to direct us into spiritual truths. This awareness becomes a tool to teach how to use their gifts. Bring truthfulness, honesty, and act in loving ways.

Help your child to self-excel in life, bringing true meaning to purpose, and raising the vibration and awareness for all.

Have you ever noticed that when fear is absent or acknowledged and released, there is the world before you to experience, no stopping, and a spring in your steps that propels you forward? Remember your connection to the Spirit of Life itself. Maybe your smile becomes so engaging it lifts those around you.

We know by scientific proof that raising one's vibrational frequency can increase the energy vibration of over 500 people. Even though we are individuals, we are all one, interconnected by and with Source. When we allow the Universal Divine flow, to move through us, we ignite the Light within to shine out to all and within all.

8

Blessing

It was a day of celebration; I was receiving my First Communion. All dressed in white with a veil. It had been raining earlier that morning, and I was to be there early to meet in my classroom with the other children. My dad drove me to the church. Once parked, he came around to the other side of the car door to carry me so my shoes would not get muddy. He asked if it was ok to shut the door. I thought, what an odd question.

As he shut the car door, the corner of the door cut the top of my right hand. The blood never dripped out of the wound. When I was in Church looking at my hand, I could see the blood so clearly coming up from the middle of the two-inch cut and coiling apart back into the wound. I was so amazed because what was out of the norm was happening. It was a very spiritual event, an awareness, and a blessing.

What we take as a fluke in life can be a beautiful lesson right before our human eyes. Even today, that memory sweeps a veil of peace over me.

What IS, is even the smallest or simplest thing we can overlook that would dim our shining Light if you feel it is below you to pay attention. We are within this beautiful energy of Light that supports and fills us with all our needs. Why would one dim or step out of the Light? You say life happens, right? You have free will to make a higher choice if you choose... Just saying.

One day somebody told me about a family who had recently rented a house and how one night the family's little boy was woken by a boy spirit shaking his bed, and things were flying around his bedroom, which greatly frightened him. A group of trees near the house that the boy could see from his bedroom window also scared him. The boy said because something terrible was there. His mother told me she also sensed awful energy. I told her about my friend that did house clearings and gave her my friend's phone number.

The spiritual clearer went out and did clearings in, around the house and yard. There were no reported happenings again.

How did the mother handle this? Wisely. She shared her concerns, gathered the needed information, and acted on it with respect, Love, and well-being for her family and self.

Why do I tell you about this happening? I want you to be aware of low vibrational energy and how it can show up in different forms, a reason to learn about raising vibration, protecting yourself, and allowing the graces of the Creator within to guide you. Use meditation, prayer, and intention; blessing your children. Let them know you love them. Tell them they are awesome the uniqueness of the Creators Love.

Keeping your cool will help teach your children and give them tools to see the picture without emotional overload and to resolve issues at hand with healthy boundaries. How do you keep your cool, you ask? It is where we adults need to learn about our inner child. Where in your life were you not acknowledged, believed, trusted, loved, a victim of abuse in any form, pushed aside, told you weren't wanted or worthy of anything, not good enough, unsupported, made to grow up too fast, lived in fear of punishment, belittled, heard conversations you did not understand, yet, it may have been a perception you soaked up making you feel unworthy? Does your child trigger your lost inner child to retaliate in outrage and then cause the cycle of your emotions to transmit onto your child?

I invite you to pick up a mirror and say to yourself; I love you. I am sorry. (Here mention all the emotional, mental, physical, and spiritual pain you have experienced in your life). Then say, please forgive me, I love you, thank you and be grateful. Now, tell your inner child how much you love them, and you will always be there for them. Call back your inner loving power, set healthy boundaries knowing you are the I am in the Creator's Divine energies.

Live

Children are in a high state of awareness.
Allow yourself to see Beauty through their eyes.
Embrace and awaken your inner child.

Remember and become once again in the awareness of love, joy,
simplicity, compassion, and amusement.

9

Music

Did you know that music can change the mood, personality, and actions of all? Even the Earth and, yes, the Universe. We are all connected by sound, vibration, and energetically. Air, water, Light, all vibrational and electrical. So why would you not stop and think before you act! I had bought a book, "All I SEE is a PART of ME." My grandchild's favorite picture was the silhouette of a child, and the whole Universe was inside the child. My grandchild was only 5yr old and understood. It was an ah-ha moment for me.

Every day we have an abundance of ah-ha moments, yet, we overlook them, forgetting our inner child. We become of the world with lost sharp boundaries belonging to the ego. Change your internal perceptions. Allow the Light of your connection of and with Source. Then you change the outcome of your canvas, your life.

My youth was shy in making close friends. I was somewhat outgoing and lost in a world that seemed at times foreign.

Some of my saving graces traveled to the beach or mountains, away from people's density, noise, and negativity. It was at the water's edge, which I felt so at home. Experiencing the sun, sea, air, surf, and bird sounds is an incredible feeling of freedom, music to my soul. It was a time to reconnect, learn, and experience in my energy field, helping me let go and release the overwhelming emotional drama I felt from others. In my later adult years, I became more aware of my empathic abilities and how to use all my gifts. One of my skills was feeling with such Love to others, not the Love a human life usually experiences. Love of all creation, to see Spirit within all connections. The earlier years of my life were from my spiritual guides teaching me. People did not talk much about ESP abilities in the Church or otherwise, and you did not want the government to know. You needed to be a kid, not treated like you were out of the norm.

Others just hide behind the veil of distorted truth. Spirit is always within and around you, waiting for you to awake to the real you, the Truth and Love of I Am.

Seek and Observe

Express and live your soul's purpose.
Allow your heart to jump with joy
as you let go of other's plans for you.
Follow your hopes and dreams,
compare you life but only unto your own.

Be the guiding Light, casting shadows away, basking in the Light of
Truth and Love.

10

Strength of awareness, hear me now.

My dad was an alcoholic and would hit my mom. Why did she stay with him that long? Fear? Too close to the picture of her canvas to see the truth? Unable to be receptive to receive the blessings of strength to change? We are so in a dream, thinking if we try being what others want, they will change, and life will change for the better. We are the only ones that can change, making better choices for ourselves. What are we teaching our children? Pictures are worth 1000 words. Have you heard the saying? Beliefs and emotions are easily transmitted from adults to children, even within the womb. When willing to review your life as an observer, ask yourselves why? What happened in my life that I would hold onto fear? How old was I? What emotional energy experience in the past affected your life of feeling unworthy, angry, doubtful, untrustworthy, abandoned, etc. Yes, all is a form of fear. How does one release the emotional bondage?

First, learn to look at yourself in a mirror and tell yourself, I Love You, I am worthy, I am sorry, I forgive myself, I am so thankful I am here, I am Light. Every day I ask for strength, for I am strength. I open my heart to receive abundant gifts to be the awareness and actions of Divine Love.

I knew a lady who had a hard time looking at herself in the mirror and say "I Love You." She made an effort for one month to look at herself in the mirror and say, I love You." An ah-ha moment happened! Her life became a newer awareness of the beautiful life within her. The events that occurred in her experience did not disappear, but a release of emotional bondage to the past. She could see how worthy and loving she truthfully was and that no one could take that away.

You do not need to give, nor should you ever give your energy/vibration away to others' manipulative actions.

Remember, you are of the Divine Love and Light, which gives you the strength to know you are, the I AM.

Have you ever heard, felt, seen, tasted, sensed, or known the vibration and sound of energy? Sure you have; we all have; you may not realize that the awareness at that moment, you took for granted. It's like breathing. Unless you are in alliance with consciousness, you only exist.

One cold Christmas night, my grandson and I went to the Christmas parade in the city, packed with excitement and entertainment. Afterward, we went into the mall to the coffee cafe to wind down from the excitement with some hot chocolate. We were both sitting in a booth drinking our hot drink, being in our quiet space, when we heard a child making sounds like I want my way. My thought was, do not come near. Ah, yes, you guess correctly? The parents came over with their child in a stroller to throw stuff away in the trash bin. That is when the little boy started to make the sounds again. Telepathically without realizing it, I told the child, "Don't Even!" The child turned his head around so quickly to look at me with giant eyes!!

I had to laugh a little because I looked at my grands, who was smiling ear to ear. I said to him, "I guess he heard me." My grandson, with his big smile, nodded his head with, "oh yes." An ah-ah moment!

Did you know? Animals, as well as all living things, are telepathic. Humans have been conditioned not to honor their telepathic abilities. It doesn't mean you can't reeducate your mind to remember. Yes, some people happen to be more open to their awareness, that's OK. Never compare yourself to another. Look within to see and to learn about your true self. You are the power of Love within. You are where you need to be at this present time, learning to be comfortable within yourself.

Give thought to what you desire. See it. Feel it and act upon the desire. Remember, children pick up on your unspoken words. Thoughts are energy, energy moves. Ensure your wanted thoughts are positive. Your child can and will pick up the vibration of your thoughts.

We all have an inner child, so this also applies to adults.

Purpose

"Fear not uncharted waters of life for I freely sail the ocean,
for what is mine to experience,
I open my arms knowing that for which
is not mine is set free for a higher purpose.
My soul yearns for the experience
to grow into a deeper connection
with the Source, the Lighthouse of my existence."

11

Choices

Life is full of challenges, choices and, opportunities. There are times we block progress intentionally and not intentionally because of old patterns, here says, fears, feelings of un-worthiness, trauma, etc., in this life and ancestral. Not bad or good, it's an awareness to see a bigger picture for change, a better outcome for you. Instead of forcing an effect, try meditation, go for a walk/hike. Go to a quiet park, mountains, or to a lake to clear self-doubt. A way to open yourself to ideas and answers that pop into your awareness of being— listen without judgment. It may take practice to see past ego blocks to bridge/connect to your inner higher understanding, which is OK. Start by listening to your breathing, making sure it is deep, slow, even, and rhythmic. After a few times engaging the routine, breathe naturally. Allow releasing stagnant low energies that serve not your higher self. Being in that understanding puts you into a productive vibration that will help all for the better.

We know what to do if we let go and listen. It's time to stop being overly busy, thinking you have to be one up on everyone else. Accept your incredible qualities. Act on those abilities and bring them out into the open. Yes, there will be critics. You can pull their drama into your energy field or smile and embrace the authentic YOU! It's not their journey.

In this changing world, listen to those who have been through ups and downs in business and personal lives. It is not about forcing an issue. It's living from a place of faith, trust, belief, Love, joy, and gratitude. It will bring a difference in your perception you had not thought to apply.

Life is living now, for we only have the now to live to its fullest. Be your Star! The Creator is waiting for your Light to shine.

"The brilliance of Love in a prism of color."

12

Intuition

What is intuition? How does it feel? What does your intuition look like from your mind's eye? Do you see color, auras? Do you sense energy within or around you? It is a knowing, no conscious reasoning. So how does a child try to describe what they are experiencing? Have you tried asking? Do you get frustrated trying to get an answer you can't understand? Remember, it is a knowing in the beautiful ability to know and amplify in one's life. "Connecting heart with creation, trust with action, experience with moving energy of molecules, atoms, light, all that is." Are divine spirits whispering guidance?

Listening to my intuition has helped me be safe, knowing before a seeable outcome. One time I was out having dinner when this uneasy feeling engulfed me. I knew I needed to go back to my hotel room. I caught a person trying to come through the window.

I see intuition as a guiding forecast from my mind's eye, not just feeling. Sometimes color can come into play, and intuitively I know what the color means.

Is that intuition when you are near something that makes you feel uneasy or excited and have no reason to understand why it just happens? Listen to your inner self, trust, and allow your child to keep that ability. To trust with understanding is a knowing; it is good. To find your intuition, first, try to quiet the mind and check within yourself.

Honor and trust your intuition. You do not need proof. You already know. There are times when speaking to another spiritual minded person will help bring the awakening you require.

Clair Senses:

Ability to perceive things, not insight. There are 8
Clair Senses:

Clair voyance, clear seeing

Clair cognizence, clear knowing

Clair audience, clear hearing

Claire empathy, clear emotional feeling

Clair sentience, clear physical feeling

Clair tangency, clear, touching

Clair salience, clear smelling

Clair gustance, clear tasting

Do you remember as a child any of these? Or now? These abilities can make a person a little edgy if not knowing how to honor and use them. Knowledge is essential to learning. Where some just allow, others require more understanding, all good.

Learning more about the Clair senses can help you connect with your abilities and understand your child without fear.

The Clair Senses are for all life, including animals, plants, trees, water, fish, birds, all energy forces. Maybe your child can talk to or hear many energies. A good source of grounding (being present is good) with the intent of keeping Love and Light within and around you. Have healthy boundaries. Come from a place of integrity. Keep vibrational energy high with truth, Love, and gratitude.

13

Dreams

We have many dreams in our life. Dreams can help us understand information from the subconscious. Dreams help us become more aware of the need to change perceptions that are not serving our purpose. I have a dream book to help me see what is going on and understand how to live my life better. Some dreams can be nightmares. What and why? If you aren't willing to learn the answers, how will you help others? Find books on the interpretation of dreams to help guide you to understand your dreams better.

Inner Child

There are many books written about your inner child. Explanation from Wikipedia: In popular psychology and analytical psychology, the term Inner child is an individual's childlike aspect. It includes what a person learned as a child before puberty.

The inner child often is conceived as semi-independent, subpersonality subordinate to the waking conscious mind.

It is the child within you that still resides.

The feeling of unworthiness, fear, unloved, trauma, etc., can stem back when you were a child.

With Hypnotherapy, Emotional and Body Code Release or, other studies, you can engage your subconscious mind to learn from feelings you brought in from your ancestry and your lifetimes. Depending on your openness and understanding, other subjects of study are always available.

There are many good books to read about the inner child, helping one reconnect to that part of yourself and allow for healing. Allow yourself to see and live a healthier life.

Example

One day, I participated in a "Spa Day" inside a health store; I enjoyed helping others feel more relaxed by doing chair massage and teaching about energy and the awareness to know and feel. Toward the end of my service time, I heard the store's phone ring and knew it was for me.

One of the employees walked over to me and said three people requesting that they meet me and are being sent over by a guru; they could be there within 30min.

I had no idea who the guru was. I said, sure, I'm having fun and can wait for them. When they arrived, the mother and her 6yr old daughter were led to me by a lady who was their guide support. The visit was for the 6yr old girl who had issues being overly introverted and pain in her back. The support lady that brought them to see me had helped the mom and daughter get out of an abusive relationship—a little history here for you. While the mother was pregnant, the father had kicked the mother twice in the stomach. The little girl witnessed abuse to the mother. The guide support got them out of harm's way of the abuser.

When they arrived at the store, the mother had the guide get a chair massage first. The mother of the child looked at me, smiling, and said, you are special. I smiled, for I did know what she was seeing. The next massage was to be for the little girl. I scanned the child's back without touching her as she was sitting on the massage chair. During the scanning of the back, she wench in pain in two different places.

I sensed the energy of her angel out in front of the massage chair. I asked the little girl if she believed in angels? Her answer was yes. I said, "can you see your angel in front of you?" Her response was, "OH, Yes." I asked, "As I scan where the pain is in your back, could you give it to your angel?" The answer was yes. The first scanning, she wrenched her back; I said, "now take a deep breath and give it to your angel." She smiled. For the second spot of pain, I had her do the same. The little girl was out of pain, full of energy, and outgoing. I am humbled and grateful for the healing that took place that day.

The trauma the little girl received while in the womb needed release. She gave the pain to her angel. That's when the Inner Child healed and, her personality changed to joy and outgoing.

How often have you or someone you knew made you or that other person feel much better with their touch? Energetic presence? What about your child or another child? Maybe, it was what the child said. Never underestimate the wisdom and abilities of children. Please, parents and guardians, help keep that wisdom of creativity blossoming in your children.

Your integrity, Love, compassion, and gratitude will be felt by your child and others. Let go of what others think. Come from the heart; look deep within your heart/soul for you truly already know. Go within, learn to see the truth. Watch how little children can let go and move on. With your Love and support accepting your child as the Light they are and remembering you too are Light so you can let go, be kind to yourself, forgive and love yourself; it is a blessing in itself. Remember the saying, "if it doesn't kill you, it makes you stronger." Integrity.

14

Creativity and Balance

What is your child's outlook on being creative? Do you or your child know the earth? The shape of leaves and plants of all kinds? Why and how do they grow, stretching toward the sun? Seeing them and touching them, not by virtual reality. Have you lost the essential elements of living? Divine energy in human form. Feel, hear, see, taste, sense, touch the earth, be grounded, and not forget the real purpose of connection. Technology is gadgets invented with information correct or not. Healthy living, human connection with physical touch will always be a critical aspect of life; you become just a gadget without you. Have you been too busy with gadgets? Learn, be life itself. Balance, teach, be, experience the senses of wonder without the need for the crutch of overuse in technical devices. Help your children be more living in the now, learning, and communicating with a human connection.

Those who can balance technology and be active in relation to others and outdoors are healthier, balanced, less stressed, and are open to remembering to engage in their inner child of wonder and play. This keeps one with a higher perspective of grounding and creativity. Balance.

Obstacles

Life brings human experiences of obstacles that block our awareness. How often have you been too close to a situation that you could not see the bigger picture? Yes, I too, more than once! I started doing my soul searching, which my awareness of learning was to observe from a nonjudgmental outlook of myself and the event/issue at hand. I gained a better picture and came from a source of awareness to accept myself by recalling I am in control to choose better outcomes, releasing the drama of thoughts, desires, wants, and commands of others upon myself. We honor ourselves when we take back our power and stand up for ourselves and take responsibility for our actions.

Living someone else's demands is turning your back on the purpose of your own life, forgetting the beauty of your creation, blinded to the Divine Light to experience great love, peace, joy, and compassion.

There is a saying, "Be like the river ever flowing over and around the rocks seizing the excitement, turmoil, and calmness, ever-flowing into the sea of wonder, beauty, and life, never-ending." Become an observer, be in the now, neutral. Be understanding, let go of judgment, for we are not the other person.

Their thoughts, reactions, beliefs, and maybe fears may block them from coming into a place of compassion and self-love. You are responsible for your actions.

"Our children learn from us; teach them wisely."

Do a life review as an observer without judgment. You may learn that even through pain, sorrow, fear, shamefulness, hate, and unworthiness, you can and will rise above. Understanding you can change by remembering who you are, Divine essence that has never left you nor stopped loving you. You have the power to overcome obstacles.

It is your choice to fall victim to others or become a unique person, seeking the Love of Spirit within you. There is only one you. Be your Divine Light, and your child will feel your Love and support, gaining compassion and Love for all creation.

As you allow your true Divine self to unfold, you allow your children to accept their uniqueness with a presence of self-love, compassion, forgiveness, and gratitude. It is never, never, never too late for change. Be in the now. Help heal the past and allow the future to unfold from a place of Love without force.

Be open to your higher consciousness; fear not to see the truth. Allow yourself once again to remember your inner child. By doing so, learn how to teach your beautiful children to be like the never-ending flowing river of self-love connected to

The Divine Creator, co-creating in harmony.

Inspirations

Feel

"Feel the energy of the Earth? Her Love, Life, and Beauty always give, always listen, teach, and support. She never judges but still works at balancing the living atmosphere and growth for a sustainable life."

How is the balance in yourself? Can you still see beauty and goodness among the chaos? Does judgment block your perception of truth?

Step away into nature. Feel the Love that is showered upon all life.

You are beauty, Spirit, and Love.

Open Arms

"I fear not uncharted waters of life, for I freely sail the ocean for what is mine to experience. I open my arms, knowing that which is not mine is set free for a Higher Purpose. My soul yearns for the experiences to grow into a deeper connection with Source, Creator of Life the Light House of my existence."

Stillness

"Still, but thy mind, allow my sense of awareness betroth to my purpose and bring to me an open heart from the sea of Love."

Embrace

"Children are in a high state of awareness. Allow yourself to see beauty through their eyes. Embrace and awaken your; Inner-Child. Remember and become once again in awareness of Love, joy, simplicity, compassion, and amusement - LIVE!"

Matter is Energy

"A time of deeper connection is happening within and through you. You are a spiritual being having a human experience. Attune your vibration through Higher Awareness healing is found within you."

Peace

"Open your heart. Shine Divine Love. Embrace the experience. See with amazement the world within."

Seeking

Seek and observe...

"Express and live your soul's purpose, your path. Allow your heart to jump with joy as you let go of others' plans for you. Follow your hopes, desires, and joy. You are here to follow your path, not someone else's. Compare your life only but to your own. Be of the guiding Light casting shadows away, basking in the Light of Love and truth. As you follow your heart's desire, freedom begins with finding and walking your Divine path."

"Art an expression of the Soul, freedom in the movement of Being."

"When you are ready you will let go of all negative thought, which keeps you from being creative. You have the power, ability and creativeness within you. Take the risk and expect the best. Change your attitude of the world within you and you change the world around you"

"Brilliance of Love in the Prism of Color"

Prayers and Wishes

"Let go, my friend, and be assured your angels are with you; ask them to help you be grounded and fully open to their guidance. You are much loved. Blessings of strength to you."

Life is full of challenges, choices, and opportunities. There are times we just block progress because of old patterns, hearsays, fears, feelings of unworthiness, and so on. Instead of forcing an outcome, one might be better to meditate, go for a walk/hike, to the park or mountains, to the water to clear the self-doubt, and open yourself to ideas and answers that pop into your awareness of being, listening without judgment. It may take practice to see past the ego bloc to bridge/connect to your higher consciousness; that is OK. We know what to do if we let go and listen.

It's time to stop being overly busy, thinking you have to be one up on everyone else. Learn to accept your incredible qualities and act on these abilities. Bring them out into the open. There will be critics, and you can pull their drama in or smile and embrace the authentic YOU! What I say here is also what I know is valuable in the changing world. Listen to others who have been through tremendous ups and downs in business, personal and spiritual living; it is not about forcing an issue; it's living with faith, trust, belief, Love, joy, gratitude, forgiveness, and willingness; ask for guidance. Life is living now, for we only have the now to live to its fullest. Be your STAR!"

"Once was a lioness who was told and treated like a clown, a no one, until she saw her reflection and realized she was so much more, the Queen of her domain and strength of the Divine."

"Let go, dear one of the hear-says, and look within yourself. You are here to co-create a life of Love, wellness, peace, and joy. Accept the Divine within you. Fear not; accept the beat of your drum in harmony with knowing you are deserving and worthy. Be the best that sings from your true heart.

Allow your Divine Higher Consciousness

to be your support and guide."

"May the World be Light and heaviness raised. May all the stars shine upon your face, and the blessings of Divine Love be your grace."

Namaste/Blessings

Lakota Prayer

Wakan Tanka, Great Mystery,

teach me how to trust

my heart,

my mind,

my intuition,

my inner knowing,

the senses of my body,

the blessings of my spirit.

Teach me to trust these things

so that I may enter my Sacred Space

and love beyond my fear.

and thus Walk in Balance

with the passing of each glorious Sun.

The Sacred Space is the space between exhalation and inhalation (contentment) from the Lakota perspective. To Walk-in Balance is to have Sky (spirituality) and Earth (physicality) in Harmony.

Snowfall of the Mind

Suggested Book Reading For Learning

All I see is a Part of Me
   By Chara M. Curtis

Totem Animals
   By Teresa Luengo Cid

The Eight Clair Senses
   By Natalie Marquis

The Indigo, Crystal, Rainbow, and Star Children
   By Judy Lipson

Your Inner Child
   By Nancy Landrum

Empath
   By Judy Driver

Reiki
   By Karen Frazier

Anatomy of the Spirit
   By Caroline Myss

The Four Agreements
  By Don Miguel Ruiz

A Course in Miracles
  By Alan Cohen

The Alchemist
  By Paulo Coelho

You Can Heal Your Life
  By Louise Hay

Change Your Thought
  By Dr. Wayne W. Dyer

Expanding your Consciousness

The Beauty of Spirit within You,

as child and adult.

Testimonials

A dear friend of mine is a loving and kind old soul who lifts the vibration of love all around her where ever she travels. She has been through many rough obstacles and still practices from a place of loving teachings. Her parents and spiritual godmother, Nana, lived and taught in the Shaman Ways.

Early as she can remember always connected and spoke to Spirit. Around the age of 5, after a car accident, she could see and witness all that is true, feel, hear, and sense the presence of Spirit.

She raised her children to live from the Spirit. Does that mean one does not go through and experience the issues and events of life? We are spirit manifested in a human body, "The Essence of All that Is Love"; experiencing. You have one body and mind in this lifetime so take care as you would take care of anything you cherished, protected, and loved.

"Your religion is in you; listen to your dreams called in from your heart." SW

Another friend and his son have the gift of communicating with animals and their needs.

A dear mother and child I have known for many years have the gift of spiritual sight.

The gifts are not to be feared. Become more aware and be in connection with your inner spirit of truth and love. Become more informed, act as a loving and proactive person. Studying how to protect yourself from others' energies can help keep you from falling into the dramas of life.

Claim back your power! Hold in high vibrations of peace, love, and compassion. The more you are thankful for your life helps bring different perspectives opening to harmony and balance. Let go of feelings and memories that pull your energy into misery; it keeps you from divine growth. "Forgiveness, gratitude, love, and compassion; honoring this brings in peace.

NOTES

NOTES

NOTES

NOTES

NOTES

Reviews

"An inspiring book to sparkle the memories of the inner child that resides in all of us and honor the sensitivity, intuition and connection of both, the sacred voices of your children and your own inner child!"

- Teresa Luengo Cid, Author of Totem Animals: Messenger Spirits of Unity

"This book is a great resource and source of inspiration for parents in supporting their children in being who they are created to be. Parents will receive support for valuing their children's abilities and encouragement to not be afraid to truly pay attention to what their children are saying. Through Sandra's stories and insights, parents will find that by reading this book, not only will their children be blessed, but parents will discover the potential to heal their inner child as well."

- Debby W.

My gratitude to all for the help and support in writing, illustrating, and printing this book.

Blessings

Made in the USA
Middletown, DE
07 May 2022